The JWeb
Accessible Siddur

Enjoy the Shabbat Service

Symbols – Hebrew – Phonetics – English

online @ jweb.org.uk

Order of Service

This Accessible Siddur is available for you to print additional copies at www.jweb.org.uk

Morning Blessings

Songs

Praying Together

Reading from the Torah

Being with our Community

Time to be with Friends & Family

Foreword

To be a real community doesn't mean attempting to make everyone conform to the same way of doing things, it means rising to the challenge set by the concept, *"Kol Yisrael arevim zeh ba zeh – all Israel are responsible for each other."* How do we demonstrate this responsibility as far as creating prayer spaces, minyanim? We have to ensure that we are creating opportunities for everyone in our congregations to access prayer in the way most appropriate for them and yet with the creation of such a service comes the responsibility to accompany people during their prayer. A minyan may not always need to be thought of as simply a number of people praying together but a true minyan would ask who needs to be in the room to ensure everyone feels valued, supported and joined in with. I hope at least four groups of people will always make up a B'yachad minyan and all four parts will feel equally valued. Whether it is adults of differing abilities, their families, carers or members of the wider community, a B'yachad service should be welcoming and accessible for all.

It is also important not to say we don't have any members who need this provision. At the first B'yachad service a lady in her 60s sat and cried throughout. During kiddush I asked her why she had found the service so emotional. She explained that she had not been to synagogue since the behaviour of her three year-old son was deemed inappropriate for services. It was her little boy now in his 40s sitting next to her – they had finally found a welcoming minyan where they could both feel comfortable in synagogue. May nobody feel excluded from shul for 40 years and may we always create prayer spaces where we can truly pray b'yachad, truly together.

Rabbi Miriam Berger
Finchley Reform Synagogue

Dedicated to Mitch Wax whose many years of volunteer-led Shabbat services at Ravenswood Village inspired us to produce this Siddur.

Shabbat Shalom

Welcome!

Shabbat

Shalom!

Shabbat Shalom – may you have
a peaceful Sabbath!

Sha-bat sha-lom!

שַׁבָּת שָׁלוֹם!

שַׁבָּת

Putting on the Talit

Baruch	Atah	Adonai	Eloheinu	Melech	ha'olam,
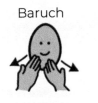					

asher	kid'shanu	b'mitz'votav	v'tzivanu	l'hitatef batzitzit.

וְצִוָּנוּ

לְהִתְעַטֵּף

We praise You, Eternal God, Sovereign of the universe: You sanctify us by Your commandments, and invite us to wrap ourselves in a Tallit.

Baruch Atah Adonai Eloheinu Melech ha'olam, asher kid'shanu b'mitz'votav v'tzivanu l'hitatef batzitzit.

בָּרוּךְ אַתָּה יְיָ אֱלֹהֵינוּ מֶלֶךְ הָעוֹלָם אֲשֶׁר קִדְּשָׁנוּ בְּמִצְוֹתָיו, וְצִוָּנוּ לְהִתְעַטֵּף בַּצִּיצִת.

People choose to wear a tallit to help us feel closer to God and to help us think about our prayers. There are fringes or tassels on each of the four corners and these are put there to remind us of all of Gods commandments. Did you know that there are 613 commandments and not just 10?

Modeh Ani:
I Give Thanks to You

Modeh ani lefanecha,	Melech chai vekayam,	shehechezarta be	nishmati b'chemla,	B'chemlah,	b'chemlah,
Rabah emunatecha,	Rabah emunatecha.				

I give thanks to You, Ruler of all life,
for You have returned my soul to me
in mercy. Great is Your faithfulness.

Modeh ani lefanecha,
Melech chai vekayam,
Shehechezarta be nishmati
b'chemlah,
b'chemlah,
b'chemlah,
Rabah emunatecha,
Rabah emunatecha.

מוֹדָה אֲנִי לְפָנֶיךָ,
מֶלֶךְ חַי וְקַיָּם,
שֶׁהֶחֱזַרְתָּ בִּי נִשְׁמָתִי
בְּחֶמְלָה, בְּחֶמְלָה
רַבָּה אֱמוּנָתֶךָ, רַבָּה אֱמוּנָתֶךָ.

We can say this prayer every morning when we wake up. Today we say it together. When we say this prayer, we are thanking God that we wake up every day. It is nice for us to remember to say thank you for good things.

What are you thankful for today?

Morning Blessings

Baruch

Atah

Adonai

Eloheinu

Melech

ha'olam,

asher

natan

lesechvi

vinah

lehavchin

bein yom

uvein laylah.

We praise you, Eternal God, Sovereign of the universe, you rule both space and time; you taught the rooster to tell day from night.

Baruch Atah Adonai Eloheinu, Melech ha'olam asher natan lasechvi vinah lehavchin bein yom uvein layla.

בָּרוּךְ אַתָּה יְיָ אֱלֹהֵינוּ מֶלֶךְ הָעוֹלָם אֲשֶׁר נָתַן לַשֶּׂכְוִי בִינָה לְהַבְחִין בֵּין יוֹם וּבֵין לָיְלָה.

Elohai Neshama

Elohai,	Elohai	n'shamah
Shenatata	bi	t'horah hi.

Atah	v'rata	Atah	y'tzartah

Atah	n'fachtah bi

V'Atah	m'sham'rah	m'sham'rah	b'kir'bi.

My God, the soul You have given me is pure. You created it, You formed it, You breathed it into me, and You guard it while it is within me.

Elohai, Elohai n'shamah
Shenatata bi t'horah hi. (x2)

Atah v'ratah, Atah y'tzartah,
Atah n'fachtah bi,
V'Atah m'sham'rah, m'sham'rah
b'kir'bi.

אֱלֹהַי, אֱלֹהַי נְשָׁמָה
שֶׁנָּתַתָּ בִּי טְהוֹרה הִיא. (x2)

אַתָּה בְרָאתָהּ, אַתָּה יְצַרְתָּהּ, אַתָּה
נְפַחְתָּהּ בִּי,
וְאַתָּה מְשַׁמְּרָהּ, מְשַׁמְּרָה בְּקִרְבִּי.

This prayer is another chance for us to say thank you to God for giving each of us a special and wonderful soul.

Hallelu: Let Us Praise God

Hallelu,   hallelu,   hallelu,   hallelu,   hallelu,   hallelu.

Hallelu-El   b'kod'sho,   Halleluhu   birkiya u'zo.

Halleluhu   big'vurotav,   halleluhu   k'rov gud'lo.   Hallelu...

Halleluhu   b'teika shofar,   Halleluhu   b'neivel vechinor.

Halleluhu   b'tof   umachol.

Halleluhu   b'minim   v'ugav.   Hallelu...

   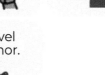

Halleluhu   b'tsil'ts'lei shama,   Halleluhu   b'stil'ts'lei t'rua.

Kol haneshama   tehallel-Yah   halleluyah.

Hallelu...   halleluyah.

Hallelujah – Praise God! Give praise to God in God's holy place, praise in God's mighty heavens, praise for God's powerful deeds, praise for God's surpassing greatness. Give praise to God with the shofar blast; praise with the lyre and harp, praise with drums and dancing, praise with the lute and pipe. Give praise to God with the clash of cymbals, praise with the clanging cymbals. Let everything that has breath praise God. Hallelujah – Praise God!

Hallelu, hallelu, hallelu,
Hallelu, hallelu, hallelu. (x2)
Hallelu-El b'kod'sho,
Halleluhu birkiya u'zo.
Halleluhu big'vurotav,
Halleluhu k'rov gud'lo.
Hallelu…
Halleluhu b'teika shofar,
Halleluhu b'neivel vechinor.
Helleluhu b'tof umachol,
Halleluhu b'minim v'ugav.
Hallelu…
Helleluhu b'tsil'ts'lei shama,
Halleluhu b'tsil'ts'lei t'rua.
Kol haneshama tehallel-Yah hallelu,
Hallelu halleluyah.

הַלְלוּהוּ בְּתֵקַע שׁוֹפָר,
הַלְלוּהוּ בְּנֵבֶל וְכִנּוֹר:
הַלְלוּהוּ בְתֹף וּמָחוֹל,
הַלְלוּהוּ בְּמִנִּים וְעוּגָב:
הַלְלוּ ...
הַלְלוּהוּ בְצִלְצְלֵי־שָׁמַע,
הַלְלוּהוּ בְּצִלְצְלֵי תְרוּעָה:
כֹּל הַנְּשָׁמָה תְּהַלֵּל יָהּ,
הַלְלוּ, הַלְלוּיָהּ:

הַלְלוּ, הַלְלוּ, הַלְלוּ,
הַלְלוּ, הַלְלוּ, הַלְלוּ (x2)
הַלְלוּ־אֵל בְּקָדְשׁוֹ
הַלְלוּהוּ בִּרְקִיעַ עֻזּוֹ:
הַלְלוּהוּ בִּגְבוּרֹתָיו
הַלְלוּהוּ כְּרֹב גֻּדְלוֹ:
הַלְלוּ ...

Hallelu is from the Book of Psalms. It tells us that there are many different ways to show that we want to say thank you to God including with music and dancing!

Am Yisrael Chai:
The Jewish People Live

Am Yisrael   chai,   am Yisrael   chai,

Am Yisrael,   am Yisrael,   am Yisrael,   chai.

Od Avinu,   chai,   Od Avinu,   chai.

Od Avinu,   Od Avinu,   Od Avinu,   chai.

The Jewish people live! Our Father in heaven lives!

Am Yisrael chai, am Yisrael chai,
Am Yisrael, am Yisrael, am Yisrael chai.
Am Yisrael, am Yisrael, am Yisrael chai. (x4)

Od Avinu chai, od Avinu chai,
Od Avinu, od Avinu, od Avinu chai.
Od Avinu, od Avinu, od Avinu chai. (x4)

עַם יִשְׂרָאֵל חַי, עַם יִשְׂרָאֵל חַי

עַם יִשְׂרָאֵל, עַם יִשְׂרָאֵל, עַם יִשְׂרָאֵל חַי

עַם יִשְׂרָאֵל, עַם יִשְׂרָאֵל, עַם יִשְׂרָאֵל חַי (x4)

עוֹד אָבִינוּ חַי! עוֹד אָבִינוּ חַי!

עוֹד אָבִינוּ, עוֹד אָבִינוּ, עוֹד אָבִינוּ חַי!

עוֹד אָבִינוּ, עוֹד אָבִינוּ, עוֹד אָבִינוּ חַי!

This song is a very happy song about the Jewish people being alive and well!

Hineh Mah Tov:
How Good It Is

Hineh mah tov	u'mah na'yim,	shevet	achim	gam yachad.

How good and pleasant it is that people live together in peace. (Psalm 133:1)

Hineh ma tov u'mah na'yim, shevet achim gam yachad. (x2)

Hineh ma tov, shevet achim gam yachad. (x2)

הִנֵּה מַה־טּוֹב וּמַה־נָּעִים שֶׁבֶת אַחִים גַּם־יָחַד. (x4)

הִנֵּה מַה־טּוֹב, שֶׁבֶת אַחִים גַּם־יָחַד. (x4)

This song is from Psalm 133. We sing about how great it is when we all try to be nice to each other and don't fight. It is lovely when we all live in peace!

מַה־טּוֹב

Havah Nagilah:
Let Us Rejoice

Havah Nagilah

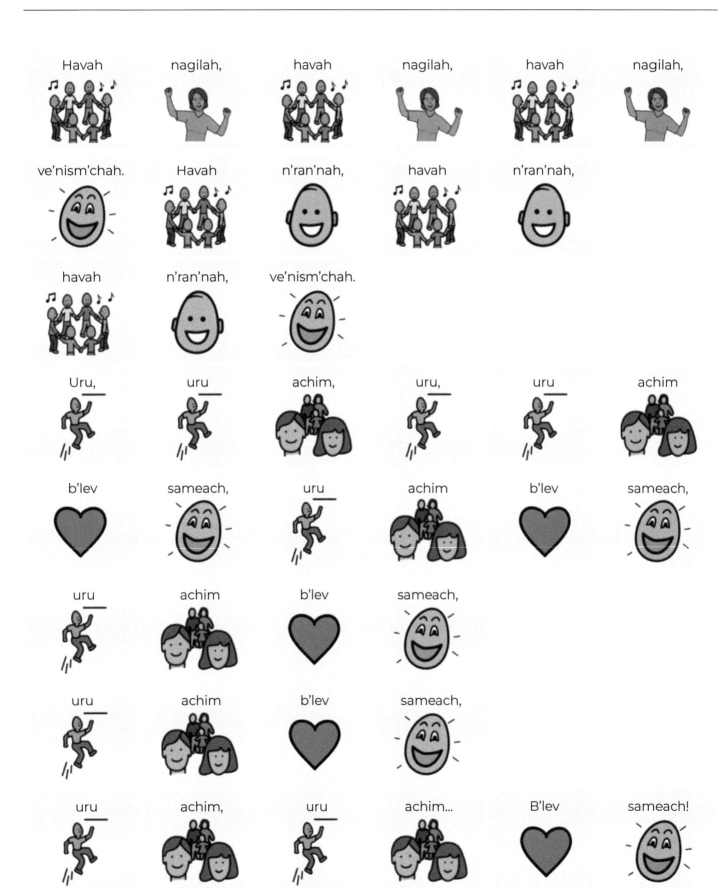

Let us be glad and rejoice! Let us sing joyfully! Awake, friends, with a joyful heart!

Havah nagilah, havah nagilah,
Havah nagilah ve'nism'chah. (x2)

Havah n'ran'nah, havah n'ran'nah,
hava n'ran'nah ve'nism'chah. (x2)

Uru, uru achim, uru, uru achim
b'lev sameach,
Uru achim b'lev sameach,
Uru achim b'lev sameach,
Uru achim b'lev sameach, uru
achim, uru achim...
B'lev sameach!

הָבָה נָגִילָה, הָבָה נָגִילָה, הָבָה נָגִילָה
וְנִשְׂמְחָה (x4)

הָבָה נְרַנְּנָה, הָבָה נְרַנְּנָה, הָבָה
נְרַנְּנָה וְנִשְׂמְחָה (x4)

עוּרוּ, עוּרוּ אַחִים, עוּרוּ אַחִים בְּלֵב
שָׂמֵחַ, עוּרוּ אַחִים בְּלֵב שָׂמֵחַ, עוּרוּ
אַחִים בְּלֵב שָׂמֵחַ, עוּרוּ אַחִים בְּלֵב
שָׂמֵחַ, עוּרוּ אַחִים..., עוּרוּ אַחִים...
בְּלֵב שָׂמֵחַ!

This song was written in 1915. It's about singing and being happy!

David	Melech	Yisrael	Chai,	chai,	v'kayam.

David, the king of Israel, lives on in the heart of our people.

David Melech Yisrael,
Chai, chai v'kayam.

דָּוִד מֶלֶךְ יִשְׂרָאֵל חַי חַי וְקַיָּם!

Lots of people love this song! Did you know that in ancient times in Israel, the words of the song were used as a code to tell people that there was a new moon? A new moon in the sky was the old way of telling us when the new Jewish month had started!

Kochi:
Not by Might

Children sing, children dream,

Though their tears may fall you can hear them call,

And another song will rise,

And another song will rise,

And another song will rise.

Not by might and not by power,
but by My spirit alone shall people
all live in peace.

Children sing, (la la la la),
children dream,
Though their tears may fall
you can hear them call,
And another song will rise,
And another song will rise,
And another song will rise.

This song is about how we should believe in living peacefully.
Caring for each other is more important than being stronger
or more powerful than someone else.

Bar'chu:
The Call to Pray Together

Bar'chu	et-Adonai	ha'mevorach!

Baruch	Adonai	ha'mevorach

L'olam va'ed,	l'olam va'ed!

Bless the Living God whom we are called to bless. Blessed is the Living God whom we are called to bless forever and ever.

Bar'chu et-Adonai ha'mevorach!
Baruch Adonai ha'mevorach
L'olam va'ed, l'olam va'ed!
Lai, lai, lai...

בָּרְכוּ אֶת יְיָ הַמְבֹרָךְ.
בָּרוּךְ יְיָ הַמְבֹרָךְ לְעוֹלָם וָעֶד,
לְעוֹלָם וָעֶד.

We are now ready to start the next part of our Shabbat service with some very special prayers and the reading of the Torah scroll!

Mah Rabu:
How Great are Your Deeds

Mah Rabu

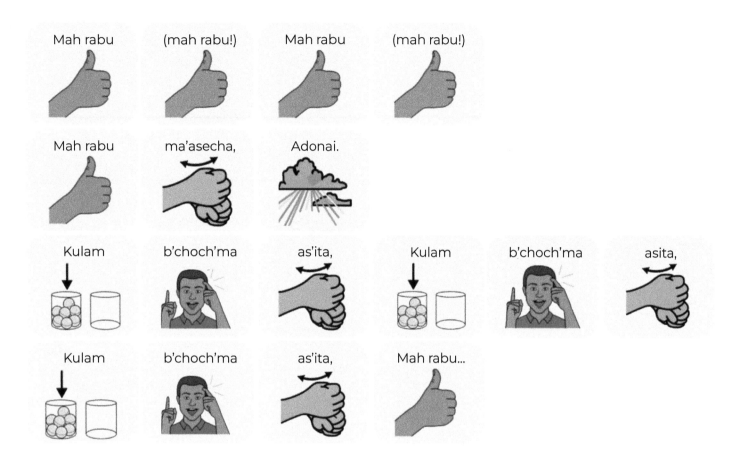

Mah rabu   (mah rabu!)   Mah rabu   (mah rabu!)

Mah rabu   ma'asecha,   Adonai.

Kulam   b'choch'ma   as'ita,   Kulam   b'choch'ma   asita,

Kulam   b'choch'ma   as'ita,   Mah rabu...

מַעֲשֶׂיךָ מַה רַבּוּ

How great are Your works, Adonai,
in wisdom You have made them all.

Mah rabu (mah rabu!)
Mah rabu (mah rabu!)
Mah rabu ma'asecha, Adonai.

Kulam b'choch'ma as'ita,
Kulam b'choch'ma as'ita,
Kulam b'choch'ma as'ita,
Mah rabu...

מָה־רַבּוּ

מָה־רַבּוּ

מָה־רַבּוּ מַעֲשֶׂיךָ, יְהוָה.

כֻּלָּם בְּחָכְמָה עָשִׂיתָ,
כֻּלָּם בְּחָכְמָה עָשִׂיתָ,
כֻּלָּם בְּחָכְמָה עָשִׂיתָ,
מָה־רַבּוּ...

מָלְאָה הָאָרֶץ קִנְיָנֶךָ:

This is from Psalm 104. This song talks about how God thought carefully and wisely about creating everything in the world. This means that each one of us is important and that we should also think about how beautiful the world is.

Yotzeir Or:
Creating Light and Dark

Yotzeir Or

Baruch	Atah	Adonai	Eloheinu	Melech	ha'olam,

yotzeir or	u'vo'rei choshech,	Oseh	shalom,	u'vo'rei	et ha'kol.

We praise You, our ever present God, Ruler of all, Maker of light and Creator of darkness, Maker of peace and Creator of all things.

Baruch Atah Adonai, Eloheinu, Melech ha'olam, yotzeir or u'vo'rei choshech, Oseh shalom, u'vo'rei et ha'kol.

בָּרוּךְ אַתָּה יְיָ, אֱלֹהֵינוּ מֶלֶךְ הָעוֹלָם, יוֹצֵר אוֹר, וּבוֹרֵא חֹשֶׁךְ, עֹשֶׂה שָׁלוֹם וּבוֹרֵא אֶת הַכֹּל.

We know how important the sun and light are to life on the planet. This prayer thanks God for creating light and dark – because both are important – and for creating peace.

The Shema:
Affirmation of Faith

Sh'ma	Yisrael	Adonai	Eloheinu 	Adonai	echud:
Baruch	Sheim kevod,	Sheim kevod,	mal'chuto	l'olam va'ed.	
Ve'ahavta	et Adonai	Elohecha, 	b'chol-levavecha,	uv'chol-nafshecha	uvechol – meodecha
v'hayu hadvarim haeleh	asher anochi	m'tzavecha	hayom, al levavecha	v'shinantam	l'vanecha
v'dibarta bam,	b'shivtecha b'veitecha,	uv'lechtecha vaderech	uv'shochvecha,	uv'kumecha:	Uk'shartam le'ot al yadecha,
v'hayu l'totafot bein einecha,	uchetavtam al muzezot	beitecha uvisharecha.			

Hear, O Israel: The Eternal One is our God, the Eternal God is One.

Praised forever be God's glorious majesty.

Sh'ma Yisrael: Adonai Eloheinu, Adonai echud: (Say this out loud)

Baruch Sheim kevod, Sheim kevod mal'chuto l'olam va'ed. (Say this in a whisper)

Ve'ahavta et Adonai Elohecha, b'chol-levavecha, uv'chol-nafshecha, uvechol-meodecha:

V'hayu hadvarim haeleh asher anochi m'tzavecha hayom, al levavecha v'shinantam l'vanecha v'dibarta bam, b'shivtecha b'veitecha, uv'lechtecha vaderech, uv'shochvecha, uv'kumecha:

Uk'shartam le'ot al yadecha, v'hayu l'totafot bein einechah, uchetavtam al mezuzot, beitecha uvisharecha.

(say this out loud) שְׁמַע יִשְׂרָאֵל יְיָ אֱלֹהֵינוּ, יְיָ אֶחָד:

(say this in a whisper) בָּרוּךְ שֵׁם כְּבוֹד מַלְכוּתוֹ לְעוֹלָם וָעֶד.

וְאָהַבְתָּ אֵת יְיָ אֱלֹהֶיךָ בְּכָל-לְבָבְךָ וּבְכָל-נַפְשְׁךָ וּבְכָל-מְאֹדֶךָ:

וְהָיוּ הַדְּבָרִים הָאֵלֶּה אֲשֶׁר אָנֹכִי מְצַוְּךָ הַיּוֹם עַל-לְבָבֶךָ:

וְשִׁנַּנְתָּם לְבָנֶיךָ וְדִבַּרְתָּ בָּם בְּשִׁבְתְּךָ בְּבֵיתֶךָ וּבְלֶכְתְּךָ בַדֶּרֶךְ וּבְשָׁכְבְּךָ וּבְקוּמֶךָ:

וּקְשַׁרְתָּם לְאוֹת עַל-יָדֶךָ וְהָיוּ לְטֹטָפֹת בֵּין עֵינֶיךָ:

וּכְתַבְתָּם עַל-מְזֻזוֹת בֵּיתֶךָ וּבִשְׁעָרֶיךָ:

The Shema is one of the most important prayers in all of Judaism. If we are able to, we say the first line with our eyes closed and one hand in front of our eyes. The second line is said very quietly.

The Amidah:
The Standing Prayer

| Adonai | s'fatai | tiftach, | ufi yagid | t'hilatecha. |

God, open my lips and may my mouth say Your praises.

Adonai, s'fatai tiftach, ufi yagid t'hilatecha.

אֲדֹנָי שְׂפָתַי תִּפְתָּח וּפִי יַגִּיד תְּהִלָּתֶךָ.

In synagogue, anyone who is able to stand will stand for this prayer. This prayer is said quietly to ourselves. There may be times during the prayer when some people bow. This is one of the most important prayers in the synagogue service. It is also sometimes called the Shemoneh Esrei which means 18 in Hebrew. This is because it originally had 18 blessings in it but now has 19!

In the Amidah we remember how good God is. We ask God to help us feel better and be healthy and safe. We finish the Amidah by thanking God for the good things we have.

אֲדֹנָי

שְׂפָתַי

תִּפְתָּח

Oseh Shalom:
Prayer for Peace

Oseh shalom

bimromav,

Hu ya-aseh shalom

aleinu

V'al kol Yisrael

ve'al kol b'nei adam

Yaseh shalom,

Yaseh shalom,

Shalom aleinu

ve'al kol Yisrael

v'imru

im'ru

amen.

Maker of peace from above,
make peace for us, for all Israel,
and for everyone.

Oseh shalom bimromav,
Hu ya-aseh shalom aleinu
V'al kol Yisrael, ve'al kol b'nei adam.

Yaseh shalom, yaseh shalom,
Shalom aleinu, ve'al kol Yisrael. (x2)

Ve'imru, im'ru amen.

עֹשֶׂה שָׁלוֹם בִּמְרוֹמָיו הוּא יַעֲשֶׂה שָׁלוֹם עָלֵינוּ וְעַל כָּל יִשְׂרָאֵל, וְעַל כָּל בְּנֵי אָדָם.
יַעֲשֶׂה שָׁלוֹם, יַעֲשֶׂה שָׁלוֹם, שָׁלוֹם עָלֵינוּ וְעַל כָּל יִשְׂרָאֵל.

This prayer is a very well known song in Judaism! Here we use it to finish the Amidah – the standing prayer.

Reading from the Torah:
Learning from our Teaching

Al shlosha d'varim

Al shlosha d'varim,

Al shlosha d'varim,

shlosha d'varim,

Ha'olam,

Ha'olam omed.

Al ha'Torah,

v'al ha'avodah

v'al gemilut chasadim.

Civilisation depends on three things: on Torah, prayer and acts of kindness.

– Simeon the Righteous,
  Avot 1:2 (Ethics of the Fathers).

Al shlosha d'varim,
Al shlosha d'varim,
Al shlosha d'varim, shlosha d'varim,
Ha'olam, ha'olam omed. (x2)

Al ha'Torah, v'al ha'avodah,
V'al gemilut chasadim. (x2)

עַל שְׁלֹשָׁה דְבָרִים,

עַל שְׁלֹשָׁה דְבָרִים,

עַל שְׁלֹשָׁה, שְׁלֹשָׁה דְבָרִים

הָעוֹלָם, הָעוֹלָם עוֹמֵד. (x4)

עַל הַתּוֹרָה וְעַל הָעֲבוֹדָה

וְעַל גְּמִילוּת חֲסָדִים. (x4)

We are now ready to take the Torah scroll out from the Ark so that we can read this week's portion which is also known as a Parasha. Everyone who is able to stands when the Torah scrolls are carried to the Bimah.

Prayer before the Reading from the Torah

Reading from the Torah

Bar'chu

et-Adonai

ha'mevorach

Baruch

Adonai

ha'mevorach

le'olam va'ed.

Baruch

Atah

Adonai

Eloheinu

Melech

ha'olam,

asher

bachar banu

mikol ha'amim

v'natan lanu

et Torato.

Baruch

Atah

Adonai,

notein

haTorah.

38

1. Bless the One whom
   we are called to bless.

2. Blessed is the Living God,
   whom we are called to bless
   forever and ever.

3. Blessed are You, our Living God,
   Sovereign of the universe,
   who chose us from all people
   to give us Your Torah.

4. Blessed are You God, who gives
   us the Torah.

1. Bar'chu et Adonai ha'mevorach

2. Baruch Adonai ha'mevorach
   l'olam va'ed.

3. Baruch atah Adonai Eloheinu
   Melech ha'olam, asher bachar
   banu mikol ha'amim, v'natan
   lanu et Torato.

4. Baruch Atah Adonai,
   notein haTorah.

בָּרְכוּ אֶת יְיָ הַמְבֹרָךְ:

בָּרוּךְ יְיָ הַמְבֹרָךְ לְעוֹלָם וָעֶד:

בָּרוּךְ אַתָּה יְיָ אֱלֹהֵינוּ מֶלֶךְ הָעוֹלָם,

אֲשֶׁר בָּחַר בָּנוּ מִכָּל הָעַמִּים וְנָתַן

לָנוּ אֶת תּוֹרָתוֹ:

בָּרוּךְ אַתָּה יְיָ, נוֹתֵן הַתּוֹרָה.

These are the blessings before we read from the Torah scrolls. Someone on the Bimah will say the lines numbered 1 and 3. Everyone who is able to and wants to says the lines numbered 2 and 4.

אַתָּה

Dvar Torah:
Torah Study

D'var

Torah

דְּבַר תּוֹרָה

Prayer after Reading from the Torah

Reading from the Torah

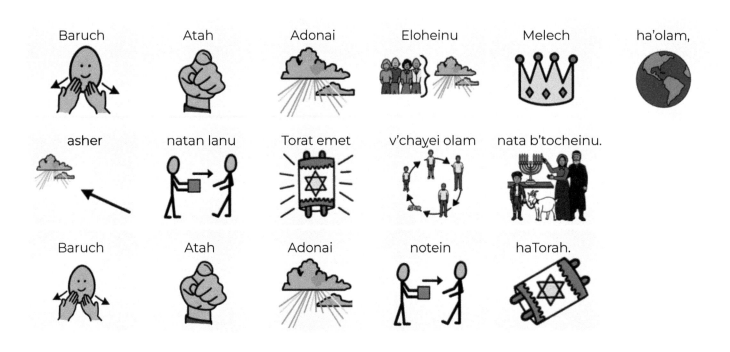

Baruch   Atah   Adonai   Eloheinu   Melech   ha'olam,

asher   natan lanu   Torat emet   v'chayei olam   nata b'tocheinu.

Baruch   Atah   Adonai   notein   haTorah.

42

Blessed are You, our Living God, Sovereign of the universe, who gave us the teaching of truth and planted eternal life within us, Blessed are You God, who gives us the Torah.

Baruch Atah Adonai Eloheinu Melech ha'olam, asher natan lanu Torat emet, v'chayei olam nata b'tocheinu.

Baruch Atah Adonai, notein haTorah.

בָּרוּךְ אַתָּה יְיָ אֱלֹהֵינוּ מֶלֶךְ הָעוֹלָם, אֲשֶׁר נָתַן לָנוּ תּוֹרַת אֱמֶת, וְחַיֵּי עוֹלָם נָטַע בְּתוֹכֵנוּ: בָּרוּךְ אַתָּה יְיָ, נוֹתֵן הַתּוֹרָה.

These are the blessings after we have read the Torah scrolls. These will be said or sung by the person on the Bimah. Lots of people might want to say Amen at the end of the blessing.

Prayer for the Royal Family

Prayer

Royal Family

Our God who gives salvation to kings and queens and dominion to princes, whose kingdom is an everlasting kingdom – may You bless:

Our Soveriegn Lady, Queen Elizabeth,
Philip, Duke Of Edinburgh,
Charles, Prince Of Wales,
And All The Royal Family.

May the supreme Eternal in Your mercy preserve the Queen in life, guard her and deliver her from all trouble and sorrow. May You bless and protect Her Majesty's Armed Forces. May You put a spirit of wisdom and understanding into her heart and into the hearts of all her counsellors, that they may uphold the peace of the realm, advance the welfare of the nation, and deal kindly and justly with all the House of Israel. In her days and in ours may our Eternal God spread the tabernacle of peace over all the dwellers on earth; and may the redeemer come to Zion; and let us say Amen.

Prayer for the Welfare of the State of Israel and its Defence Forces

State of Israel

Prayer

State of Israel

May the Eternal who blessed our fathers Abraham, Isaac and Jacob and our mothers Sarah, Rebekah and Leah bless the State of Israel, its leaders and advisors in the land which You swore unto our ancestors to give us. Put into their hearts the love and fear of You to uphold it with justice and righteousness, and may we be worthy in our days to witness the fulfilment of the words of Your servants, the prophets: "For out of Zion shall go forth the Law and the word of the Lord from Jerusalem."

Eternal God: Remember the Israel Defence Forces, guardians of our Holy Land. Protect them from all distress and anguish, and send blessing and success to all the work of their hands. Grant peace in Your Holy land and everlasting happiness to all its inhabitants, so that Jacob shall again have peace and tranquillity, with none to make him afraid. Spread the tabernacle of Your peace over all the dwellers on earth. May this be Your will; and let us say, Amen.

Eitz Chayim:
Tree of Life

Shalom,

Shalom.

Eitz chayim hi

l'ma'chazikim ba,

v'tom'che'ha

me'ushar

Shalom,

Shalom.

It's a tree of life to those who grasp it,
And those who uphold it are happy.

Shalom, shalom (x4).

Eitz chayim hi l'ma'chazikim ba,
V'tom'che'ha me'ushar.

Shalom, shalom (x4).

שָׁלוֹם, שָׁלוֹם (x4)

עֵץ חַיִּים הִיא לַמַּחֲזִיקִים בָּהּ

וְתֹמְכֶיהָ מְאֻשָּׁר

שָׁלוֹם, שָׁלוֹם (x4)

The Torah scroll is now returned to the Ark while we sing this song.
Everyone who is able to stands up when the Torah scroll is carried back
to the Ark. Some people like to touch or kiss the Torah with their tallit
or siddur as it goes past them.

Torah Torah

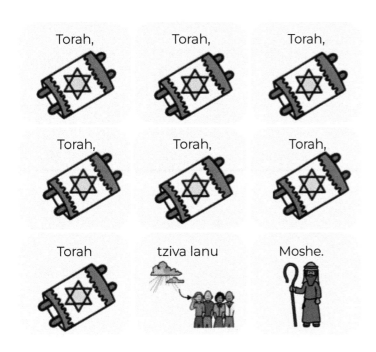

Torah, Torah, Torah,

Torah, Torah, Torah,

Torah tziva lanu Moshe.

רַחֲמִים

עָלֶיהֶ

Moses commanded to us the Torah.

Torah, Torah, Torah,
Torah, Torah, Torah,
Torah tziva lanu Moshe.

This song is a very happy song about how Moses gave us the Torah from God.

Refuah Shlemah:
Prayer for Healing

Mi Sheberach

Avoteinu:

Avraham,

Yitzchak,

v'Ya'akov,

v'Imoteinu:

Sarah,

Rivka,

Rachel.

v'Leah,

Hu yivarech

virapei

et hacholeh

et hacholah,

ben

bat.

May the Source of strength, Who blessed the ones before us, help us find the courage to make our lives a blessing. And let us say: Amen.

Bless those in need of healing, with refuah shlemah: the renewal of body, the renewal of spirit. And let us say: Amen.

Mi Sheberach
Avoteinu: Avraham, Yitzchak, v'Ya'akov,
v'Imoteinu: Sarah, Rivka, Rachel, v'Leah,
Hu yivarech virapei

et hacholeh/hacholah _____
ben/bat _____

מִי שֶׁבֵּרַךְ אֲבוֹתֵינוּ וְאִמּוֹתֵינוּ, אַבְרָהָם, יִצְחָק וְיַעֲקֹב, שָׂרָה, רִבְקָה, רָחֵל וְלֵאָה, הוּא יְבָרֵךְ אֶת הַחוֹלִים [names]. הַקָּדוֹשׁ בָּרוּךְ הוּא יִמָּלֵא רַחֲמִים עֲלֵיהֶם, לְהַחֲלִימָם וּלְרַפֹּאתָם וּלְהַחֲזִיקָם וּלְהַחֲיוֹתָם, וְיִשְׁלַח לָהֶם מְהֵרָה רְפוּאָה, רְפוּאָה שְׁלֵמָה מִן הַשָּׁמַיִם, רְפוּאַת הַנֶּפֶשׁ, וּרְפוּאַת הַגוּף, הַשְׁתָּא בַּעֲגָלָא וּבִזְמַן קָרִיב. וְנֹאמַר: אָמֵן.

During this prayer for healing, we quietly think about anyone we know or love who isn't well and we pray for them to get better soon.

Aleinu:
The Future is Up to Us

Aleinu

Sha...Dai

Al kein	n'kaveh	l'cha,

Al kein	n'kaveh	l'cha,

Al kein	n'kaveh	l'cha,

Adonai	Eloheinu

Lirot	m'heirah	b'tiferet uzecha	l'takein	olam.

Lirot	m'heirah	b'tiferet uzecha	b'malchut	Shaddai.

54

Therefore, we put our hope in You, Eternal One our God, that we may soon behold the glory of Your might, perfecting the world under the sovereignty of God.

Sha…Dai dada dai dai dai

Al kein n'kaveh l'cha,
Al kein n'kaveh l'cha,
Al kein n'kaveh l'cha Adonai Eloheinu. (x2)

Lirot m'heirah b'tiferet uzecha l'takein olam.
Lirot m'heirah b'tiferet uzecha b'malchut Shaddai…

שַׁדַּי, דַּד דַּי דִּי דַּי דִּי...
עַל כֵּן נְקַוֶּה לְּךָ, עַל כֵּן נְקַוֶּה לְּךָ, עַל
כֵּן נְקַוֶּה לְּךָ, יְיָ אֱלֹהֵינוּ (x2)
לִרְאוֹת מְהֵרָה בְּתִפְאֶרֶת עֻזֶּךָ, לְתַקֵּן
עוֹלָם
לִרְאוֹת מְהֵרָה בְּתִפְאֶרֶת עֻזֶּךָ,
בְּמַלְכוּת שַׁדַּי ...

In this prayer we hope that in the future, everyone will be good to each other and trust in God.

Yesh Kochavim:
There are Stars

Yesh kochavim

she'oram

magi'a artzah,

Rak ka'asher heym atzmam

avdu v'eynam.

Yeish anashim

she'ziv

zichram

mei'ir

Ka'asher heym atzmam

einam od b'tocheinu

Orot eyleh

ha'mavhikim

b'cheshkat ha'lailah.

Hem, hem

she'mar'im l'adam

et ha'derech

et ha'derech.

There are stars up above, so far away
we only see their light long, long
after the star itself is gone.

And so it is with people that we've
loved – their memory keeps shining
ever brightly though their time with
us is done.

But the stars that light up the
darkest sky, these are the lights
that guide us.

As we live our days these are the ways,
we remember, we remember. (x2)

Yeish kochavim she'oram magi'a
artzah,
Rak ka'asher heym atzmam avdu
v'eynam.
Yeish anashim she'ziv zichram mei'ir
Ka'ashar heym atzmam einam od
b'tocheinu.
Orot eyleh ha'mavhikim b'cheshkat
ha'lailah.
Hem, hem she'mar'im l'adam
et ha'derech, et ha'derech. (x2)

יֵשׁ כּוֹכָבִים שֶׁאוֹרָם
מַגִּיעַ אַרְצָה רַק כַּאֲשֶׁר
הֵם עַצְמָם אָבְדוּ וְאֵינָם.
יֵשׁ אֲנָשִׁים שֶׁזִּיו זִכְרָם
מֵאִיר כַּאֲשֶׁר הֵם עַצְמָם

אֵינָם עוֹד בְּתוֹכֵנוּ. אוֹרוֹת
אֵלֶּה הַמַּבְהִיקִים בְּחֶשְׁכַּת
הַלַּיְל הֵם שֶׁמַּרְאִים
לָאָדָם אֶת הַדֶּרֶךְ.

This is from a beautiful poem by Hannah Senesh. Hannah Senesh
was a very brave Jewish woman who saved lots of people's lives in
the Second World War.

This poem which we are singing today helps us think about the
people who we love but are no longer with us.

Mourners' Kaddish

Yitgadal	v'yitkadash	sh'mei rabah.	B'alma	di'v'ra chirutei	v'yamlich malchutei
b'chayeichon uv'yomeichon	uv'chayei d'chol beit Yisrael	ba'agala uvizman kariv,	v'imru	"Amen."	
Y'hei sh'mei rabah	m'varach	l'alam ul'almei almaya.			
Yitbarach v'yishtabach	v'yitpa'ar v'yitromam	v'yitnaseh, v'yithadar	v'yitaleh v'yithalal	sh'mei d'kudsha.	B'rich Hu.
L'eila	min kol birchata	v'shirata	tush'b'chata 	v'nechemata	d'amiran
b'alma,	v'imru:	"Amen." 			
Y'hei sh'lama raba	min shmaya	v'chayim aleinu	v'al-kol-Yisrael	v'imru:	Amen.
Oseh shalom	bimromav	Hu yaseh shalom	aleinu	v'al kol-Yisrael,	v'al kol b'nei adam,
v'imru:	"Amen."				

Glorified and sanctified be God's great name throughout the world which He has created according to His will.

May He establish His kingdom in your lifetime and during your days, and within the life of the entire House of Israel, speedily and soon; and say, Amen.

May His great name be blessed forever and to all eternity. Blessed and praised, glorified and exalted, extolled and honored, adored and lauded be the name of the Holy One, blessed be He, beyond all the blessings and hymns, praises and consolations that are ever spoken in the world; and say, Amen.

May there be abundant peace from heaven, and life, for us and for all Israel; and say, Amen.

He who creates peace in His celestial heights, may He create peace for us and for all Israel; and say, Amen.

Yitgadal v'yitkadash sh'mei rabah. B'alma di-v'ra chirutei, v'yamlich malchutei b'chayeichon uv'yomeichon uv'chayei d'chol beit Yisrael, ba'agala uvizman kariv, v'imru: "Amen."

Y'hei sh'mei rabah m'varach l'alam ul'almei almaya.

Yitbarach v'yishtabach, v'yitpa'ar v'yitromam v'yitnaseh, v'yithadar v'yitaleh v'yithalal sh'mei d'kudsha. B'rich Hu. L'eila min kol birchata v'shirata, tush'b'chata v'nechemata d'amiran b'alma, v'imru: "Amen."

Y'hei sh'lama raba min shmaya v'chayim aleinu v'al kol Yisrael, v'imru: "Amen."

Oseh shalom bimromav, hu yaseh shalom aleinu v'al kol Yisrael, v'al'kol-b'nei'adam, v'imru: "Amen."

יִתְגַּדַּל וְיִתְקַדַּשׁ שְׁמֵהּ רַבָּא.
בְּעָלְמָא דִּי בְרָא כִרְעוּתֵהּ, וְיַמְלִיךְ
מַלְכוּתֵהּ בְּחַיֵּיכוֹן וּבְיוֹמֵיכוֹן וּבְחַיֵּי
דְכָל בֵּית יִשְׂרָאֵל. בַּעֲגָלָא וּבִזְמַן
קָרִיב וְאִמְרוּ אָמֵן:
יְהֵא שְׁמֵהּ רַבָּא מְבָרַךְ לְעָלַם
וּלְעָלְמֵי עָלְמַיָּא:

יִתְבָּרַךְ וְיִשְׁתַּבַּח, וְיִתְפָּאַר וְיִתְרוֹמַם
וְיִתְנַשֵּׂא וְיִתְהַדָּר וְיִתְעַלֶּה וְיִתְהַלָּל
שְׁמֵהּ דְּקֻדְשָׁא בְּרִיךְ הוּא לְעֵלָּא מִן
כָּל בִּרְכָתָא וְשִׁירָתָא, תֻּשְׁבְּחָתָא
וְנֶחֱמָתָא, דַּאֲמִירָן בְּעָלְמָא, וְאִמְרוּ
אָמֵן:

יְהֵא שְׁלָמָא רַבָּא מִן שְׁמַיָּא וְחַיִּים
עָלֵינוּ וְעַל כָּל יִשְׂרָאֵל, וְאִמְרוּ אָמֵן:
עֹשֶׂה שָׁלוֹם בִּמְרוֹמָיו הוּא יַעֲשֶׂה
שָׁלוֹם עָלֵינוּ וְעַל כָּל יִשְׂרָאֵל, וְעַל
כָּל בְּנֵי אָדָם, וְאִמְרוּ אָמֵן:

The Kaddish prayer is said by anyone who is mourning the death of a loved one. Although the prayer looks like it is in Hebrew, it is actually in a language called Aramaic. Kaddish means Holy and the prayer reminds us that God is good and helps to create peace.

Shalom Chaverim:
Goodbye Friends, See You Soon!

Shalom chaverim,

Shalom chaverim,

Shalom, Shalom.

L'hitra'ot, L'hitra'ot.

Shalom, Shalom.

לְהִתְרָאוֹת

Shalom chaverim,
Shalom chaverim,
Shalom, shalom.

L'hitra'ot, l'hitra'ot,
Shalom, shalom.

שָׁלוֹם חֲבֵרִים,
שָׁלוֹם חֲבֵרִים,
שָׁלוֹם שָׁלוֹם.
לְהִתְרָאוֹת, לְהִתְרָאוֹת,
שָׁלוֹם, שָׁלוֹם.

This song is about saying goodbye and see you soon to our friends as the Shabbat service is nearly over!

Adon Olam:
Master of the Universe

Adon olam,

asher

Malach,

B'terem kol

y'tsir nivra.

L'et na'asah

v'cheftso kol,

Azai Melech,

sh'mo nikra.

V'acharei

kichlot ha'kol.

L'vado

yim'loch nora.

V'hu hayah,

v'hu hoveh,

V'hu yih'heh

b'tifara.

Eternal God who ruled alone before creation of all forms, at whose desire all began and as the Sovereign was proclaimed. Who, after everything shall end alone, in awe, will reign, who was and is for evermore, the glory that will never change.

Adon olam, asher Malach,
B'terem kol y'tsir nivra.
L'et na'asah v'cheftso kol,
Azai melech sh'mo nikra.

V'acharei kichlot ha'kol,
l'vado yim'loch norah.
V'hu hayah, v'hu hoveh,
v'hu yih'heh b'tifara.

אֲדוֹן עוֹלָם אֲשֶׁר מָלַךְ,
בְּטֶרֶם כָּל יְצִיר נִבְרָא.
לְעֵת נַעֲשָׂה בְחֶפְצוֹ כֹּל,
אֲזַי מֶלֶךְ שְׁמוֹ נִקְרָא.

וְאַחֲרֵי כִּכְלוֹת הַכֹּל,
לְבַדּוֹ יִמְלוֹךְ נוֹרָא.
וְהוּא הָיָה, וְהוּא הֹוֶה,
וְהוּא יִהְיֶה, בְּתִפְאָרָה.

This famous Shabbat service song has been a part of synagogue services since the 15th Century! Adon Olam is about how God lives forever and about how God is there to look after us every day. There are lots of different tunes for this song – which is your favourite?

אֲדוֹן עוֹלָם אֲשֶׁר מֶלֶךְ

Kiddush

Baruch

Atah

Adonai

Eloheinu

Melech

ha'olam,

borei

p'ri hagafen.

We praise You, Eternal God,
Sovereign of the universe,
Creator of the fruit of the vine.

Baruch Atah, Adonai, Eloheinu
Melech ha'olam, borei p'ri hagafen.

בָּרוּךְ אַתָּה יְיָ אֱלֹהֵינוּ מֶלֶךְ הָעוֹלָם,
בּוֹרֵא פְּרִי הַגָּפֶן.

We have now finished the Shabbat service and are ready to say the
Kiddush blessings over the wine or grape juice.

Ha'motzi

Baruch	Atah	Adonai	Eloheinu	Melech	ha'olam,

ha'motzi lechem	min ha'aretz

We praise You, Eternal God, Sovereign of the universe, who brings forth bread from the earth.

Baruch Atah, Adonai, Eloheinu Melech ha'olam, hamotzi lechem min ha'aretz.

בָּרוּךְ אַתָּה יְיָ, אֱלֹהֵינוּ מֶלֶךְ הָעוֹלָם, הַמּוֹצִיא לֶחֶם מִן הָאָרֶץ.

We are now ready to say the blessing over the challah. We hope you enjoyed this Shabbat service – Shabbat Shalom!

הַמּוֹצִיא

JWeb's Resource Pack
for your Inclusive Shabbat

JWeb has produced a pack of free online resources which are designed to inspire and support inclusion in synagogues. Our Inclusion Campaign includes a downloadable copy of this Accessible Siddur (printed copies are available to synagogues and community leaders), a film of a model Reform Synagogue Shabbat service and a practical toolkit, packed with ideas and inspiration.

This campaign is the result of our research and consultation with learning disability professionals, rabbis, parents, carers and people with learning disabilities. Please spread the word by encouraging everyone to take a look. Let's make our communities more inclusive and bring the joy of Shabbat to everyone with learning disabilities.

Visit www.jweb.org.uk to use our resources pack.
Do you have something to share with our community?
Contact us at jweb@jweb.org.uk.

If you have finished using this siddur – don't throw it away! Siddurs are a special kind of book that we don't destroy. If you have printed out extra copies, or your copy is worn out please ask your rabbi to help you to dispose of the book (or printed pages) respectfully.

Compiled by Deborah Gundle and Anna Perceval

*With thanks to the many people who have contributed to this
siddur and who enjoy an inclusive and diverse community.*

Angela Goodman
Cantor Zoe Jacobs
David Bash
East London and Essex Liberal Synagogue
Finchley Reform Synagogue
Gateways: Access to Jewish Education
Gesher School
Honey Aharon

Langdon
Leor Harel
Leeds Jewish Welfare Board
Mich Sampson
Mitch Wax
Norwood
Rabbi Charley Baginsky
Rabbi David Mason
Rabbi Debbie Young-Somers
Rabbi Laura Janner-Klausner
Rabbi Miriam Berger
Rabbi Richard Jacobi
Rythmn & Jews
Sharon Daniels
Shoshanna Bloom
Shulamit Morris-Evans
The Breakaway Committee
The Fed
The Seneca Trust
Tony Babot

Design: hope.agency

J.Web